G000094560

F. Adams

Geeky Jokes

By F. Adams

Contents

Introduction

Blessed are the geeks, for they shall inherit the earth!

In less enlightened times being labelled a geek was often pejorative, but in the 21st century geeks, particularly science and technology geeks, have become essential players in any business that seeks to compete in today's fast paced market - it's *finally* cool to be a geek!

This book contains over 600 science and technology themed jokes, which might require a little subject matter expertise to fully appreciate, but even if you don't get them straight away you may well still learn something interesting *and* funny to expand your geekspertise.

Archaeology

Why did the archaeologist go bankrupt?

Because his career was in ruins.

At University I studied archaeology.

I scraped through my exams.

After a long excavation, an Egyptologist had a pain in her lower back.

She had to go and see a cairopractor!

Archaeologists are fickle.

They're always dating other people.

What did Richard III say when a planning proposal was submitted for building a car park.

"Over my dead body"

What do you call a neolithic man taking a walk?

A meanderthal.

Most parents tell their daughters to marry doctors.

I told mine to marry an archaeologist because the older she gets, the more interested he will be in her.

Archaeology is the science that proves you can't keep a good man down.

Ever since my brother got his archaeology degree, all he's done is have a dig.

Aside from criminology, I'd say archaeology is the profession with the highest body count.

Show me an archaeologist, and I'll show you a man who practices skull drudgery.

My archaeological research has been called ground breaking.

Astronomy

What was the name of the first satellite to orbit the Earth?

The moon

How do you know when the moon is going broke?

It's down to its last quarter.

In awe, I watched the waxing moon ride across the zenith of the heavens like an ambered chariot towards the ebony void of infinite space, wherein the tethered belts of Jupiter and Mars hang forever festooned in their orbital majesty.

And as I looked at all this I thought: "I really must put a roof over this toilet".

Copernicus' parents deserve some of the credit for his great discovery.

Apparently at the age of twelve they said to him: "Young man, when are you going to realize that the world does NOT revolve around you."

How many astronomers does it take to change a light bulb?

Eight:

1. One observational astronomer to measure luminosity and redshift of bulb.
2. One theoretical astronomer to calculate spherical co-ordinates of bulb.
3. One departmental head to write to PPARC, for project funds.
4. One astronomical engineer to design and build the bulb replacing satellite.
5. One starling SIG programmer to write satellite control and data reduction software.
6. One NASA mission control expert to arrange satellite launch and say "t-2 go for main engine start." etc.
7. One remote observer to manipulate the satellites arm once in elliptical orbit around light bulb.
8. One Grad student to act as scapegoat in event of mission failure.

The density of Saturn is so low that the whole planet would float on the water in your bath?

You wouldn't want to try this experiment at home though, as it would leave a massive ring.

How does the astronomer cut his hair? Eclipse it.

What do you call an alien with three eyes?

An aliiien!

What happened to the astronaut who stepped on chewing gum?

He got stuck in Orbit!

One day on Mercury lasts about 1408 hours.

The same as one Monday on Earth.

How many astronomers does it take to change a light bulb?

Ten! One to change the bulb, and nine to argue how their own bulb gives better colour.

How many light bulbs does it take to screw up an astronomer?

I was up all night wondering where the Sun had gone, then it dawned on me.

Biology

What do you get when you cross a cow with an octopus?

A meeting with the ethics committee and swift removal of your research funding.

How many tickles does it take to make a squid laugh?

Ten-tickles.

A muscle fibre walks into a bar and says, "Landlord! A pint of your finest adenosine triphosphate!"

The barman replies, "That'll be 80p."

Biology is the only science in which multiplication is the same thing as division.

Health is merely the slowest rate at which one can die.

Life is a sexually transmitted disease.

How many biologists does it take to change a light bulb?

Four. One to change it and three to write the environmental impact statement.

What did the biologist couple name their twins?

One was called Jessica and the other one was Control.

What was the biologist wearing on her first date?

Designer genes.

An infectious disease walks into a bar. The bartender says, "We don't serve your kind in here."

The disease replies, "Well, you're not a very good host."

Why does formic acid neutralize all other acids?

Because it's ant-acid.

Evolution is God's way of issuing upgrades.

Sign on the door of the microbiology lab:

"Staph Only!"

What do you call a place of worship made out of amino acids?

A cysteine chapel!

What did the femur say to the patella?

I kneed you.

A man accidentally ingested some alpha-L-glucose and discovered that it had no ill effect.

Apparently he was ambidextrose.

What's the difference between a dog and a marine biologist?

One wags a tail and the other tags a whale.

If tomato is a fruit, does that make ketchup a smoothie?

Why didn't the dendrochronologist get married?

All he ever dated was trees!

Two cows are walking through the pasture.

One cow says, "Have you heard about this mad cow disease? Are you worried?"

The other cow replies, "Why should I worry? I'm a rabbit."

Two cows are walking through the pasture.

One cow says, "Have you heard about this mad cow disease? Are you worried?"

The other cow replies, "Holy %#%$! A talking cow!"

What do you call a snake after it drinks five cups of coffee?

A hyper boa.

Where does a hippopotamus go to university?

Hippocampus.

Pavlov is sitting in a bar when the phone rings.

"Damn!" he shouts, " I forgot to feed the dog."

Why was Pavlov's hair so soft?

Classical conditioning

"Day 19, I have successfully conditioned my master to smile and write in his book every time I drool."

What do you get when you cross a mosquito with a rock climber?

Nothing. You can't cross a vector and a scalar.

Did you hear about the microbiologist who travelled to thirty different countries and learned to speak six languages?

He was a man of many cultures.

How does Juliet maintain a constant body temperature?

Romeostasis.

Why did the bacterium cross the microscope?

To get to the other slide.

"Today," said the professor, "I will be lecturing about the liver and spleen."

Up in the gallery, one medical student leaned toward the other, "Damn, if there's one thing I can't stand it's an organ recital."

Entomology really bugs me!

I don't know what carbon dating is, but I'll try anything at this point

We just hired a molecular biologist… Man, is he small.

What do you call two crows on a branch?

Attempted murder.

What's a biologists definition of a graph?

An animal with a long neck.

Why did the two algae never have sex?

Because they had a planktonic relationship.

What does seaweed say when it's stuck at the bottom of the sea?

"Kelp! Kelp!"

What's a comb jelly's favourite time of day?

It's 10:04.

Why do seagulls fly over the sea?

Because if they flew over the bay they would be called bagels!

A blowfly goes into a bar and asks, "Is that stool taken?"

What do lawyers and sperm have in common?

A one in 3,000,000 has a chance of becoming a human being.

How many evolutionists does it take to change a light bulb?

Only one, but it takes eight million years.

What do you call a fish that operates on brains?

A neurosturgeon.

If a plant is sad do the other plants photosympathise?

Clones are people two!

Two blood cells met and fell in love. Alas, it was all in vein.

The problem with the gene pool is that there is no lifeguard.

A student was so poor that all he could afford to rent was someone's outhouse.

A few weeks later he was asked how he was doing.

He said, "Great, I've sub-let my basement to a microbiologist!"

What do retroviruses cause?

Saturday night fever.

Two fish swim into a concrete wall.

One turns to the other and says dam!

Why did the bacterium cross the road?

To prove he wasn't chicken.

Do biologists take cellfies?

Food poisoning can B. Cereus.

A red blood cell walks into a busy restaurant.

The hostess asks, "Would you like to sit at the bar?"

The red cell answers, "No thanks, I'll just circulate."

What does Staphylococcus Aureus and David Attenborough have in common?

They both produce Biofilms.

What do you give some one who's got everything?

Penicillin!!!!

I envy microbiologists.

Their problems are very small.

In an interesting paradox...

Noses run but feet smell.

Microbiology grows on you.

Chemistry

What is the most important rule in chemistry?

Never lick the spoon!

Wanna hear a joke about sodium hydride?

NaH.

Wanna hear a joke about potassium?

K.

How can you spot a chemist in the bathroom?

They wash their hands before they go.

There was a time I used to tell a lot of Chemistry jokes.

Now I only do it periodically.

Cole's law: thinly sliced cabbage.

Two chemists go to a café for lunch.

The waiter takes their drink order.

First Chemist says, "I think I'll have an H2O."

Second chemist says, "I'll have H2O too."

When they drink them the second chemist keels over.

Mary was a chemist
but Mary is no more
what Mary thought was H2O
was H2SO4

What do you do with a dead chemist?

Barium.

What do you call a periodic table with gold missing?

Au revoir.

If you're not part of the solution, you're part of the precipitate.

What do you call a tooth in a glass of water?

A one molar solution.

How many moles are in a bowl of guacamole?

Avocado's number.

What do you get if you have Avogadro's number of donkeys?

Molasses.

Got mole problems? Call Avogadro at 602-1023

Why was the mole of oxygen molecules excited when he walked out of the singles bar?

He got Avogadro's number!

What was Avogadro's favourite sport?

Golf - because he always got a mole-in-one.

What did Argon do when Copper insulted him?

Argon had no reaction.

Did you hear about the chemist who was reading a book about Helium?

He just couldn't put it down.

What kind of ghosts haunt chemistry faculties?

Methylated spirits.

How did the chemist survive the famine?

By subsisting on titrations.

Why did the acid go to the gym?

To become a buffer solution!

What is a cation afraid of?

Dogions!

What did the bartender say when oxygen, hydrogen, sulphur, sodium, and phosphorous walked into his bar?

OH SNaP!

What do you call an educated tube?

A graduated cylinder.

What did the thermometer say to the graduated cylinder?

"You may have graduated, but I've got many degrees."

What did you do with Element 43 last night?

None of your Bismuth.

Why did the noble gas cry?

Because all his friends Argon.

My dog is made of calcium, nickel and neon?

He's a CaNiNe.

Did you hear about the industrialist who had a huge chloroform spill at his factory?

His business became insolvent.

Why did the bear dissolve in water?

It was a polar bear.

According to a chemist, why is the world so diverse?

Because it's made up of alkynes of people.

What do dipoles say in passing?

"Have you got a moment?"

Why are chemists great for solving problems?

They have all the solutions.

If the Silver Surfer and Iron Man were to team up, they'd be alloys.

A mosquito was heard to exclaim,

That a chemist had poisoned her brain.

The cause of her sorrow

was para-dichloro-

diphenyltrichloroethane

An organic chemist goes into a shop.

Chemist: "Hey, you got any of that inhibitor of 3-phosphoshikimate-carboxyvinyl transferase?

Shopkeeper: "You mean Roundup?"

Chemist: "Yeah, that's it. I can never remember that dang name."

My chemistry experiment blew up?

Oxidants happen!

Why did Carbon marry Hydrogen?

They bonded well from the minute they met.

The optimist sees the glass half full.

The pessimist sees the glass half empty.

The chemist sees the glass completely full, half with liquid and half with air.

How can you tell the difference between a chemist and a plumber?

Ask them to pronounce unionized.

Why did the employer force his employees to walk between high-voltage plates before entering the work place?

Because he didn't want any unionized workers.

Oxygen and Magnesium went out on a date?

OMg!

Nitrogen asked Oxygen out on a date.

She said NO!

What happened to the man who was stopped for having sodium chloride and a nine-volt in his car?

He was booked for a salt and battery.

What do you get if you swap the carbon atoms in a benzene ring for iron atoms?

You get a ferrous wheel.

Why did the chemist sole and heel his shoes with silicone rubber?

To reduce his carbon footprint.

I asked the guy sitting next to me if he had any Sodium Hypobromite.

He said NaBrO

What is the show cesium and iodine love watching together?

CsI

Did you hear about the man who got cooled to absolute zero?

He's 0K now.

What kind of fish is made out of 2 sodium atoms?

2 Na

How do Sulphur and Oxygen communicate?

A sulphone.

I Used To Be Obsessed With Chromatography

Now I realise it was just a phase.

Why did the army need all the acid?

To neutralise the enemy base.

Sixteen sodiums walk into a room followed by Batman.

Scientists say the universe is made up of protons, neutrons and electrons.

They forgot to mention morons.

My dad's sister was a rich chemist.

When she died I got all the antimony.

Dubstep titration:

Drop the base.

Do these protons make my mass look big?

A Hug without U is just toxic.

Ice is a polar molecule.

I studied exothermic reactions before they were cool.

Computers and Programming

Do you know why Facebook went public?

They couldn't figure out the privacy settings!

Man is the best computer we can put aboard a spacecraft...

and the only one that can be mass produced with unskilled labour.

What did Al Gore play on his guitar?

An Algorithm.

There's a band called 1023 MB

They haven't got any gigs yet.

What is another name for a computer virus?

A terminal illness.

I wonder what my parents did to fight boredom before the Internet.

I asked my 17 brothers and sisters and they didn't know either.

I changed my password to "incorrect"...

So whenever I forget what it is the computer will say "Your password is incorrect."

My mother said that if I don't get off my computer and do my homework she'll slam my head on the keyboard, but I think she's
jokinfjreoiwjrtwe4to8rkljreun8f4ny84c8y4t58lym4wthylmhaw

How does a network administrator greet people who come to his house?

Welcome to 127.0.0.1

Supercomputer: what it sounded like before you bought it.

I put a hex on 57005 people and now they're dead.

A computer lets you make more mistakes faster than any invention in human history, with the possible exceptions of handguns and tequila.

A computer once beat me at chess, but it was no match for me at kick boxing.

Moses had the first tablet that could connect to the cloud.

Keyboard not connected, press F1 to continue.

I accidentally fell asleep smoking an e-cigarette and when I woke up my whole house was on the internet.

Artificial intelligence is usually no match for real stupidity.

The truth is out there. Anybody got the URL?

Never underestimate the bandwidth of a truck full of tapes hurtling down a hill.

To err is human and to blame it on a computer is even more so.

Some things Man was never meant to know. For everything else, there's Google.

If you think patience is a virtue, try surfing the net on a 14.4k dial up connection.

A Life? Cool! Where can I download one of those from?

Annie Key always regretted taking computer class.

What kind of doctor fixes broken websites?

A URLologist.

I think there is a duck in my router. It always goes NAT, NAT, NAT.

I was going to tell you a UDP joke, but you wouldn't get it.

Hello, would you like to hear a TCP joke?

Yes, I'd like to hear a TCP joke.

OK, I'll tell you a TCP joke.

OK, I'll hear a TCP joke.

Are you ready to hear a TCP joke?

Yes, I am ready to hear a TCP joke.

OK, I'm about to send the TCP joke. It will last 10 seconds, it has two characters, it does not have a setting, it ends with a punchline.

OK, I'm ready to hear the TCP joke that will last 10 seconds, has two characters, does not have a setting and will end with a punchline.

I'm sorry, your connection has timed out.

Hello, would you like to hear a TCP joke?

I could tell you an ICMP joke, but it would probably be repetitive.

I'll tell you a DNS joke but be advised, it could take up to 24 hours for everyone to get it.

Knock knock.
Who's there?
SYN flood.
SYN flood who?
Knock knock....

IPv4 address space walks into a bar and yells:

"One strong CIDR please, I'm exhausted!"

A Linux geek started working at McDonalds.

A customer asked him for a Big Mac so Linux guy gave him a bit of paper with FF:FF:FF:FF:FF:FF written on it.

If Bill Gates had a penny for every time I had to reboot my computer ...oh, wait.

What is a Linux sysadmin's favourite hangout place?

Foo Bar

Unix Airlines: You walk out to the runway and they give you a box of tools and some aircraft parts.

The passengers form into groups and start building twelve different planes.

The box said 'Requires Windows Vista or better', so I installed Linux.

Windows Vista supports real multitasking, it can boot and crash simultaneously.

Failure is not an option.

It comes bundled with your Microsoft product.

Computers are like air conditioners, they stop working when you open Windows.

UNIX is basically a simple operating system, but you have to be a genius to understand the simplicity.

Unix is user friendly. It's just selective about who its friends are.

In a world without fences and walls, who needs Gates and Windows?

Viruses come in through open Windows.

Windows isn't a virus, viruses do something.

Microsoft: "You've got questions. We've got dancing paperclips."

Microsoft is not the answer. Microsoft is the question. NO is the answer.

Mac users swear by their Mac, PC users swear at their PC.

Misogynistic bash script:

unzip; strip; touch; finger; mount; fsck; more; yes; umount; sleep.

A RAID member disk walks into a bar.

The bartender asks what's wrong?

"Parity error."

"Yeah, you look a bit off."

Knock, knock.

Who's there?

<very long pause....>

Java.

There was a programmer named Gus
Who spent all his nights in a fuss.
As he lay in his bed
All that went through his head
Was (while !asleep()) sheep++;

An int, a char and a string walk into a bar and order some drinks.

A short while later, the int and char start hitting on the waitress, who gets very uncomfortable and walks away.

The string walks up to the waitress and says, "You'll have to forgive them, they're primitive types."

The programmer's wife tells him: "Run to the shop and pick up a loaf of bread. If they have eggs, get a dozen."

The programmer comes home with twelve loaves of bread.

How can you tell if a programmer is an extrovert?

When you're talking to him, he's looking at **your** shoes.

There are only two hard problems in computer science: cache invalidation, naming things, and off-by-one errors.

To understand recursion, you must first understand recursion.

A doctor, a civil engineer and a programmer are discussing whose profession is the oldest.

"Surely medicine is the oldest profession," says the doctor. "God took a rib from Adam and created Eve and if this isn't medicine I'll be…"

The civil engineer breaks in: "But before that He created the heavens and the earth from chaos. Now that's civil engineering to me."

The programmer thinks for a bit and then says: "And who do you think created chaos?"

Programming today is a race between software engineers striving to build bigger and better idiot-proof programs, and the Universe trying to produce bigger and better idiots.

So far, the Universe is winning.

If at first you don't succeed; call it version 1.0.

The beginning of the programmer's wisdom is understanding the difference between getting a program to run and having a runnable program.

Hey! It compiles! Ship it!

If Perl is the answer, you don't understand the question.

The more I C, the less I see.

If it weren't for C, we'd all be programming in BASI and OBOL.

Programming is like sex, one mistake and you have to support it for the rest of your life.

My software never has bugs. It just develops random features.

The code that is the hardest to debug is the code that you know cannot possibly be wrong.

Beware of programmers carrying screwdrivers.

Algorithm, a word used by programmers when they don't want to explain what they did.

I would love to change the world, but they won't give me the source code.

If you give someone a program, you will frustrate them for a day.

If you teach them how to program, you will frustrate them for a lifetime.

Programmers are tools for converting caffeine into code.

I'm not anti-social; I'm just not user friendly.

How many programmers does it take to change a light bulb?

None. It's a hardware problem.

My attitude isn't bad. It's in beta.

Why do programmers always mix up Hallowe'en and Christmas?

Because 31 OCT = 25 DEC.

How do you explain the movie Inception to a programmer?

Basically, when you run a VM inside another VM, inside another VM, inside another VM…, everything runs real slow!

99 Pentium chips on the wall, 99 Pentium chips, take one down, pass it around, 97.9999999999999999941218886 Pentium chips on the wall!

A SQL statement walks into a bar and sees two tables.

It approaches, and asks "may I join you?"

Three Database Admins walked into a NoSQL bar.

A little while later they walked out because they couldn't find a table.

A man flying in a hot air balloon suddenly realises he's lost.

He reduces height and spots a man down below. He lowers the balloon further and shouts to get directions, "Excuse me, can you tell me where I am?"

The man below says: "Yes. You're in a hot air balloon, hovering 30 feet above this field."

"You must work in Information Technology," says the balloonist.

"I do" replies the man. "How did you know?"

"Well," says the balloonist, "everything you have told me is technically correct, but It's of no use to anyone."

The man below replies, "You must work in management."

"I do," replies the balloonist, *"But how do you know?"*

"Well", says the man, "you don't know where you are or where you're going, but you expect me to be able to help. You're in the same position you were before we met, but now it's my fault."

What's the object-oriented way to become wealthy?

Inheritance.

Command line Russian roulette:

```
[ $[ $RANDOM % 6 ] == 0 ] && rm -rf / || echo *Click*
```

A Cobol programmer made so much money doing Y2K remediation that he was able to have himself cryogenically frozen when he died. One day in the future, he was unexpectedly resurrected.

When he asked why he was unfrozen, he was told:

"It's the year 9999 - and you know Cobol!"

Why was the JavaScript developer sad?

Because he didn't Node how to Express himself.

How many prolog programmers does it take to change a lightbulb?

Yes.

```
["hip", "hip"]
```

8 bytes walk into a bar, the bartender asks "What will it be?"

One of them says, "Make us a double."

If you put a million monkeys on a million keyboards, one of them will eventually write a Java program.

The rest of them will write Perl programs.

1f u c4n r34d th1s u r34lly n33d t0 g37 l41d.

Can you list all of the public top level domains?

ICANN

I was telling my workmates a TCP joke the other day,

I had to keep repeating it slower and slower until they got it.

How did you like my HTTP 200 joke?

It was OK.

FORTRAN is not a language, it's a way of turning a multi-million dollar mainframe into a $50 programmable scientific calculator.

C is a language that combines all the power of assembly language with all the ease-of-use of assembly language.

There was once a young man who, in his youth, professed his desire to become a great writer.

When asked to define "Great" he said, "I want to write stuff that the whole world will read, stuff that people will react to on a truly emotional level, stuff that will make them scream, cry, howl in pain and anger!"

He now works for Microsoft, writing error messages.

Autocorrect has become my worst enema.

Ubuntu is a Nguni Bantu term meaning "I can't configure Debian."

I hate audio correct.

My email password has been hacked.

That's the third time I've had to rename the cat.

I'm writing a horror screenplay.

It starts off with a ringing phone.

The person answers, and it's their mother saying "I have a computer question."

Doctor's office: All our records are electronic, now just fill out these 12 forms.

A password cracker walks into a bar. Orders a beer. Then a Beer. Then a BEER. beer. b33r. BeeR. Be3r. bEeR. bE3R. BeEr.

Caution: Do not stare into the fibre optic laser with remaining good eye.

Warning! User Error.

Please replace user and press any key to continue.

I think my neighbour is stalking me as she's been Googling my name on her computer.

I saw it through my telescope last night.

I don't care what you think you're good at, there's a 7-year-old kid on YouTube doing it better.

Where's the best place to hide a body?

Page two of Google.

A Computer Engineer was asked by his five-year-old son, "Daddy, what is Windows 95?"

He replied, "Well, it's 32-bit extensions and a graphical shell for a 16-bit patch to an 8-bit operating system originally coded for a 4-bit microprocessor, written by a 2-bit company that can't stand 1 bit of competition."

I dropped my laptop into the ocean the other day.

Now I have a Dell rolling in the deep.

How many social media marketers does it take to change a light bulb?

It's not about the change, it's about engaging people in conversations about the light bulb change.

LISP: Lots of Irritating Stupid Parentheses.

A programmer puts two glasses onto his bedside table before he goes to sleep.

A full one in case he gets thirsty during the night, and an empty one, in case he doesn't.

A Man from the toilet shouts to his wife, "Darling, darling, do you hear me?!!!!"

She replies, "What happened, did you run out of toilet paper?"

He answers, "No, restart the router, please!"

What goes "choo choo choo" while online?

Thomas the search engine.

AI technology has added real value to autocorrect.

I typed "married" the other day and it was auto-corrected to "martyred".

I never ask my kids to call me, I just change the Netflix password and then don't respond to their texts.

How do you know you've bought a bad computer?

The lower corner of screen has the words "Etch-a-sketch" on it.

The bottom left corner of my keyboard got broken.

I totally lost control!.

I asked my wife to pass me the newspaper.

She replied, "Don't be silly, borrow my iPad."

That wasp never knew what hit it!

Definitions

The following list of phrases and their definitions might help you understand the mysterious language of science, engineering and medicine.

These special phrases are particularly applicable to anyone reading a Ph.D. dissertation or academic paper.

- **It has long been known** : I didn't look up the original reference.
- **A definite trend is evident** : These data are practically meaningless.
- **While it has not been possible to provide definite answers to the questions** : An unsuccessful experiment, but I still hope to get it published.
- **Three of the samples were chosen for detailed study** : The other results didn't make any sense.
- **Typical results are shown** : This is the prettiest graph.
- **These results will be in a subsequent report** : I might get around to this sometime, if pushed/funded.
- **In my experience** : Once.
- **In case after case** : Twice.
- **In a series of cases** : Thrice.
- **It is believed that** : I think.
- **It is generally believed that** : A couple of others think so, too.
- **Correct within an order of magnitude** : Wrong.
- **According to statistical analysis** : Rumour has it.

- **A statistically oriented projection of the significance of these findings** : A wild guess.
- **A careful analysis of obtainable data** : Three pages of notes were obliterated when I knocked over a glass of beer.
- **It is clear that much additional work will be required before a complete understanding of this phenomenon occurs** : I don't understand it.
- **After additional study by my colleagues** : They don't understand it either.
- **Thanks are due to Joe Bloggs for assistance with the experiment and to Linda Andrews for valuable discussions** : Mr. Bloggs did the work and Ms. Andrews explained to me what it meant.
- **A highly significant area for exploratory study** : A totally useless topic selected by my committee.
- **It is hoped that this study will stimulate further investigation in this field** : I quit.

These phrases are applicable when reading an engineering report.

- **A number of different approaches are being tried**: We are still completely clueless.
- **An extensive report is being prepared on a fresh approach to the problem** : We have just hired three kids fresh out of college.
- **Close project coordination** : We know who to blame.
- **Major technological breakthrough** : It just about works OK, but looks very hi-tech.
- **Customer satisfaction is delivered assured** : We are so far behind schedule the customer is happy just to get it delivered.
- **Preliminary operational tests were inconclusive** : It blew up spectacularly when we threw the switch.
- **Test results were extremely gratifying** : We are so surprised that the stupid thing actually works.
- **The entire concept will have to be abandoned** : The only person who understood the thing quit.
- **It is in the process** : It is so wrapped up in red tape that the situation is about hopeless.
- **We will look into it** : Forget it! We have enough problems for now.
- **Please note** and **initial** : Let's spread the responsibility for the screw up.
- **Give us the benefit of your thinking** : We'll listen to what you have to say as long as it doesn't interfere with what we've already done.

- **Give us your interpretation** : I can't wait to hear this garbage!
- **See me** or **Let's discuss** : Come into my office, I'm lonely.
- **All new** : Parts not interchangeable with the previous design.
- **Rugged** : Far too heavy to lift!
- **Lightweight** : Lighter than "rugged".
- **Years of development** : One finally worked.
- **Energy saving** : Achieved when the power switch is off.
- **Low maintenance** : Impossible to fix if broken.

Engineering

To the optimist, the glass is half full.

To the pessimist, the glass is half empty.

To the engineer, the glass is twice as big as it needs to be.

Normal people believe that "if it ain't broke, don't fix it."

Engineers believe that "if it ain't broke, it doesn't have enough features yet."

Two engineering students crossing the campus when one said, "Where did you get such a great bike?"

The second engineer replied, "Well, I was walking along yesterday minding my own business when a beautiful woman rode up on this bike. She threw the bike to the ground, took off all her clothes and said, 'Take what you want.'"

The first engineer nodded approvingly, "Good choice; the clothes probably wouldn't fit you."

The graduate with an Engineering degree asks, "How does it work?"

The graduate with a Science degree asks, "Why does it work?"

The graduate with an Accounting degree asks, "How much will it cost?"

The graduate with an Arts degree asks, "Do you want fries with that?"

What is the difference between Mechanical Engineers and Civil Engineers?

Mechanical Engineers build weapons and Civil Engineers build targets.

When considering the behaviour of a howitzer:

A mathematician will be able to calculate where the shell will land.

A physicist will be able to explain how the shell gets there.

An engineer will stand there and try to catch it.

An engineer is walking down the road, and, seeing a frog, bends down to look at it. Suddenly, it pipes up and talks to him!

"I may look like a frog now, but I'm really a princess - if you kiss me, I'll turn back into my real self!"

The engineer smiles, picks up the frog, puts it in his (pocket protected) shirt pocket and goes on to the lab.

When he gets to the lab, he puts the frog down to get some work done, and she opens her mouth to speak:

"I tell you, I'm a beautiful princess! If you kiss me, I'll turn back, and I'll do anything you want!"

The engineer smiles, and gets on with his work. After he's done, he picks the frog up. She again starts talking to him:

"Look, I'm a princess turned into a frog! Kiss me and I'll turn into a beautiful woman. I'll do whatever you want! And I'll stay with you forever!"

The engineer peers at the frog, smiles, and tucks it back in his pocket for the walk home. When he gets there, he pulls her out, and she nearly screams at him: " **WHAT THE HELL IS THE MATTER WITH YOU?** I'm a beautiful princess, I'll do whatever you want, and I'll stay with you forever! Why won't you kiss me??"

The engineer says, "Well, I don't have time for a girlfriend, and talking frogs are way cool..."

A doctor, a lawyer, and an engineer are sentenced to death. Why is not important to the story, what is important is that the death sentence will be carried out in France - via guillotine.

The doctor is first. The executioner straps him down, hoists the glittering blade aloft, and lets it drop, whereupon it sticks about halfway down.

Now, it's a well-known tradition in capital punishment that if the execution apparatus fails for any reason, this is interpreted as a sign from God, and the death sentence is commuted. Accordingly, the doctor walks away, still very much alive.

The lawyer is next. The executioner straps him down, hoists the glittering blade aloft, and lets it drop, whereupon it sticks in the exact same spot.

Same rules apply, the lawyer walks.

The engineer is last. The executioner straps him down, as he hoists the blade aloft, the engineer twists his neck around, peers up at the blade, and says:

"Aha, I see the problem! See where the rope has jumped out of the pulley groove!"

A mathematician, scientist and engineer were tasked with finding the volume of a red ball.

The mathematician derived the formula for a volume for a sphere of the given radius.

The scientist submerged the ball in water in a graduated cylinder and measured the displaced volume.

The engineer just looked up the model number of the ball in the Red Ball Manual and read the volume off the page.

What's the difference between doctors and civil engineers?

Doctors only kill in ones.

What's the difference between a chemical engineer and a chemist?

About $50k a year.

What's the difference between a chemical engineer and a chemist?

A chemical engineer does for profit what a chemist does for fun.

How many nuclear engineers does it take to change a light bulb?

Seven. One to install the new bulb and six to figure out what to do with the old one for the next 10,000 years.

Two nuclear engineers are looking over a large nuclear power plant and one says:

"Of *course* it's perfectly safe. Any accident would be in complete violation of the guidelines established by the Federal Nuclear Regulatory Commission."

A promising young NASA aerospace engineer was killed in a horrific car accident and arrived in Heaven, protesting to St. Peter at the pearly gates. "St. Peter, I'm only 35. I'm much too young to die. I have a wonderful wife and family, so much to live for. Why in the world am I here?"

St. Peter looked through a huge stack of papers, looked over the top of his glasses and said, "Well, according to all of these hours on your time sheets, you've got to be at least 108."

Engineers will stop at nothing to avoid using negative numbers.

Two civil engineers are out hunting in the woods when one of them collapses. He doesn't seem to be breathing and his eyes are glazed.

The other guy whips out his phone and calls the emergency services. He gasps, "My friend is dead! What can I do?"

The operator says, "Calm down. I can help. First, let's make sure he's dead."

There is a silence; then a gun shot is heard. Back on the phone, the guy says, "OK, now what?"

Engineer: "Do you have any two-watt, 4-volt bulbs?"

Sales Rep: "For what?"

Engineer: "No, two."

Sales Rep: "Two what?"

Engineer: "Yes."

Sales Rep: "No."

Elastomeric insulators.

Resistance is butyl.

What did the electrical engineer say when he got shocked?

That hertz.

Looking for a boyfriend in engineering?

The odds are good, but the goods are odd.

Engineering is the art of modelling materials we do not wholly understand into shapes we cannot precisely analyse so as to withstand forces we cannot properly assess, in such a way that the public has no reason to suspect the extent of our ignorance.

How Do You Drive an Engineer Insane?

Make them watch as you fold up a road map the wrong way.

A group of NASA mechanical engineers were brainstorming how they might overcome the various thermal problems involved in sending a manned probe to the sun.

An electrical engineer overheard the discussion and said, "Why don't you just go at night?"

Games

Marriage is like a video game

Starts off easy, then gets harder, and eventually you go online and find a way to cheat.

My 14-year-old son challenged me to a game of Tekken the other day, in front of his mates.

I finished him off with a killer combo in under 30 seconds, before proudly exclaiming, "Who's your Daddy?"

He replied, "Mum says it was probably the milkman."

What does Princess Peach sit on at a bar?

A toad stool.

If there were ever to be a Minecraft movie, it would be a blockbuster.

How does Yoshi feel when he gets hurt?

Dino-sore.

My girlfriend just left me because of my overwhelming obsession with Assassin's Creed.

I tried to explain I can't Altair the past!

What do you get if you tape a stick of dynamite to a hedgehog?

Sonic **BOOM!**

What's a toilet's favorite game?

Call of Doodie.

What do you call the Nintendo Wii in France?

A Nintendo Yes.

Which video game system is always late for school?

Atardi

Why is Toad invited to every party?

Because he's a Fun-gi!

Why do Koopa-Troopas find the world so off putting?

Because they've lived a shell-tered life.

How do you get Pikachu on a bus?

You poke-em-on!

What did Wario name his art supply store?

World of Wario Crafts.

I'm a massive computer game geek, and people keep telling me to get a life.

Then I thought to myself, I don't need to get a life, I'm a gamer so I have lots of lives.

What does a gorilla wear to the beach?

A Donkey Thong.

What is Mario's favourite play?

Mamma Mia!

What did Mario use to talk to the boos?

A Luigi Board.

Why did Mario cross the road?

Because he couldn't find the warp zone!

What did the WWE Wrestler say to the video game controller?

Are you ready to rumble pack?!

What does a body building gamer use to bulk up faster?

Asteroids.

You know you're addicted to video games when you see your newborn baby and say "what a n00b!"

Why did Frogger cross the road?

Because you've been playing the game for hours and you've finally beat this level.

What was Bomberman arrested for?

Indecent Explosure.

What do you call a Pokemon who can't move very fast?

A Slow-poke.

What is Sonic the Hedgehog's favourite season?

Spring.

Why did the enderman cross the road?

He didn't, he Teleported.

How does Steve get his exercise?

He runs around the block.

While driving yesterday, I saw a banana skin in the road and instinctively swerved to avoid it.

Thanks, Mario Kart.

Did you you hear about the creeper who went to a party?

He had a **BLAST!**

I've just been playing The Sims.

My wife keeps getting into arguments because I don't have much of a social life.

My fish just died.

My son keeps coming up to me telling me he's hungry.

So I built a little square room on the side of our house and put him and my wife in it, locked the door and went back upstairs to play The Sims.

What's the difference between a mutual fund and a gamer?

The mutual fund eventually matures and starts making money!

You think YOU have bad lag?!

It took Jesus three days to respawn!

What did the minecraft turkey say?

cobble, cobble, cobble!

What do you get if you cross an American Football video game with a sick hamburger?

Madden Cow Disease.

You know you're addicted to video games when you ask your doctor how many lives you have left.

You know you're addicted to video games when your wife Zelda tells you so and your kids Mario and Luigi agree.

Video Games: Why waste good technology on science and medicine?

Geology

One tectonic plate bumped into another and said...

"sorry, my fault"

My geologist girlfriend said I was gneiss.

But then she took me for granite.

Don't expect perfection from geologists;

They all have their faults.

Geology jokes

You've got to dig them.

Why wasn't the geologist hungry?

He'd lost his apatite.

Why are geologists like hipsters?

They both like things that were underground before they became cool.

How fast does a fault move?

A mylonite.

What did the lump of coal say to the diamond?

I see you've been under a lot of pressure.

I hate geology puns.

My sediments exactly.

Plateaus are the highest form of flattery.

Schist happens.

I keep all my core samples in separate buildings to keep them from being contaminated.

I have a shed made out of wood for the shale.

I needed something sturdier to hold the basalt so it's built like a brick schist house.

Did you hear about the dishonest glaciologist?

He was caught with his hand in the till.

What is a geologists favourite movie?

Pyrites of the Caribbean.

Mountains aren't just funny, they're hill areas!

San Andreas is not my fault.

Reunite Pangaea!

Linguistics and Etymology

"I've just had the most awful time," said a boy to his friends.

"First I got angina pectoris, then arteriosclerosis. Just as I was recovering, I got psoriasis. They gave me hypodermics, and to top it all, tonsillitis was followed by appendectomy."

"Wow! How did you pull through?" sympathised his friends.

"I don't know," the boy replied. "Toughest spelling test I've ever had."

Polyamory is wrong.

Obviously you can't just mix Greek and Latin roots like that.

A Roman walks into a bar and asks for a martinus.

"You mean a martini?" the bartender asks.

The Roman replies, "if I wanted a double, I would have asked for it!"

Scientists have found that the centre of Jupiter contains the letter "i".

Caesar walks out of McDonald's and runs into Brutus.

"How were the burgers Caesar?

"Great. Ate two, Brute."

An English professor complained to the pet shop proprietor,

"The parrot I purchased uses improper language."

"I'm surprised," said the owner. "I've never taught that bird to swear."

"Oh, it isn't that," explained the professor. "But yesterday I heard him split an infinitive."

A linguist's husband walked in and caught his wife sleeping with a young student.

He said, "Why, Susan, I'm surprised."

She bolted upright, pointed her finger and corrected him, "No. I am surprised. You are astonished."

When you misspell a word the errorists win!

The village blacksmith finally found an apprentice willing to work hard for long hours.

The blacksmith immediately began his instructions to the lad, "When I take the shoe out of the fire, I'll lay it on the anvil; and when I nod my head, you hit it with this hammer."

The apprentice did just as he told. Now he's the village blacksmith.

A linguist was invited to a wedding.

The other guests looked on in horror as the Best Man made the invitation to toast the happy couple.

A childless Canadian couple decided to adopt a Mexican baby.

After they got the baby, they decided to enrol in a Spanish class.

When asked why, the wife replied, "so that when the baby starts to talk, we'll be able to understand him."

Why does monosyllabic have five syllables?

Why is abbreviated such a long word?

Recently in court, I was found guilty of being egotistical.

I am appealing.

The past, the present, and the future walked into a bar.

It was tense.

Aren't you the guy who uses contractions incorrectly?

Yes I'm

What's the difference between a hippo and a Zippo?

One is really heavy, the other is a little lighter.

I used to think I was the father of structural linguistics, but now I'm not Saussure.

What's another word for thesaurus?

Why isn't phonetic spelled the way it sounds?

Never date a tennis player.

Love means nothing to them.

I went into a book shop and asked the assistant for a book about turtles.

She asked: "Hardback?" and I said: "Yeah, and little heads."

Why are there interstate highways in Hawaii?

Let me tell you a little about myself.

It's a reflexive pronoun that means "me."

Is it possible to be totally partial?

Is there another word for synonym?

If you don't know what introspection is, you need to take a long, hard look at yourself.

What's the difference between a cat and a comma?

One marks with the claws at the ends of its paws, and the other marks a pause at the end of a clause.

You can't run in a campsite.

You have to say "ran" because it's past tents.

Where can a lexicographer always find comfort and sympathy?

In the dictionary.

In introverted lexicographer wanted to improve his success when dating, so bought a book entitled "How to Hug".

When he got it home he discovered it was volume seven of the Encyclopaedia Britannica.

Why do scientists call it research when looking for something new?

Why is it that when you transport something by car, it's called a shipment, but when it's by ship, it's called cargo?

Logic

There are only 10 types of people in the world:

Those who understand binary and those who don't.

Three logicians walk into a bar. The bartender asks, "Do all of you want a drink?"

The first logician says, "I don't know."

The second logician says, "I don't know."

The third logician emphatically says, "Yes!"

A logician's wife is having a baby. The doctor immediately hands the newborn to the father.

His wife asks impatiently: "So, is it a boy or a girl?"

The logician replies: "yes."

What do you call a logician attracted to Iron Man?

A Frege magnet.

There are only 10 types of people in the world:

Those who understand ternary, those who don't, and those who mistake it for binary.

To be, or not to be, that is the question.

"Yes" is the answer.

What is the subject of teaching to teach Boolean?

Taughtology.

Boolean Algebra

You either know it or you don't.

An octalpus has 10 arms!

Mathematics

What is the difference between a Ph.D. in mathematics and a large pizza?

A large pizza can feed a family of four.

Write the expression for the volume of a thick crust pizza with height "a" and radius "z".

What do you get when you put root beer in a square glass?

Beer.

Why did the 30-60-90 triangle marry the 45-45-90 triangle?

They were right for each other.

What do you call a teapot of boiling water on top of Mount Everest?

A high-pot-in-use.

What's the contour integral around Western Europe?

Zero, because all the Poles are in Eastern Europe!

Why did the obtuse angle go to the beach?

Because it was over 90 degrees.

What do you call a male mathematician who spent all summer at the beach?

A Tangent.

Why do you rarely find mathematicians spending time at the beach?

Because they have sine and cosine to get a tan and don't need the sun!

What do you call a mathematician's parrot that hasn't been fed?

Polly no meal.

Why is beer never served at a calculus party?

Because you shouldn't drink and derive.

What is the first derivative of a cow?

Prime Rib!

Why did you divide sin by tan?

Just cos.

Where do you bury a dead mathematician?

Asymmetry.

Why didn't the number 4 get into the nightclub?

Because he is 2 square.

4/3 people don't understand fractions.

What do you get if you cross a mathematics teacher and a clock?

Arithma-ticks!

What do you get if you cross a mathematics teacher and a magician?

Arithma-tricks!

Why can't atheists solve exponential equations?

Because they don't believe in higher powers.

Why couldn't the angle get a loan?

His parents wouldn't cosine.

How do deaf mathematicians communicate?

They use sine language.

Cakes are round, but Pi are square.

An infinite crowd of mathematicians enters a bar.

The first one orders a pint, the second one a half pint, the third one a quarter pint…

"I understand", says the bartender – and pours two pints.

Romantic relationships can actually be represented in algebra.

You for example, have definitely at some point looked at your X and asked yourself Y.

I went on a date with a chess player to an Italian restaurant with checkered table cloths.

It took him maybe half an hour to pass the salt.

Why was a student's rubber band pistol confiscated during algebra class?

It was considered a weapon of maths disruption.

2 is not equal to 3, even for very large values of 2.

The pilot and copilot of a jet aircraft are both suddenly taken ill and pass out.

Frantically, the rest of the crew attempt to find a passenger who has some flying experience.

They locate an old man who says he flew prop planes for the Polish resistance in WWII.

They take him to the cockpit and plead with him to try to fly the jet. He says "I can't do it. I'm just a simple Pole in a complex plane".

Why do plants hate mathematics?

Because it gives them square roots.

Why did the polynomial plant die?

Its roots were imaginary.

How is an artificial Christmas tree like the fourth root of -68?

Neither has real roots.

What happened to the indeterminate form that got sick?

It had to go to L'Hospital.

An engineer, a physicist, and a mathematician are tasked with using the least amount of fencing so that a herd of sheep is on the inside of the enclosure they build.

The engineer herds the sheep into small area and builds a square enclosure around them. "There", he says, "a small enclosure holding all the sheep."

The physicist proceeds to keep the sheep together and builds a circular fence around them. "A circle uses less fencing than a square."

Then it's the mathematician's turn. He builds a very small circle of fencing around himself and says, "By definition, I am on the outside."

How does one insult a mathematician?

Tell them that their brain is smaller than any $\varepsilon > 0$

Mathematics is like love; a simple idea, but it can get complex.

I have an imaginary girlfriend.

It's a complex relationship.

A task is given to an engineer, a programmer, and a mathematician. There are three buckets of water, pour the water in the barrel.

The engineer pours the first bucket in the barrel, then pours the second bucket in the barrel, then he pours the third bucket in the barrel, and he says "done".

The programmer pours the first bucket in the barrel, then he pours the second bucket in the first bucket, then he pours the third bucket in the second bucket, and he says "repeat".

The mathematician looks at the three buckets and says "A solution exists."

What do organic mathematicians throw into their fireplaces?

Natural Logs.

There are three kinds of people: those who can count and those who can't.

An engineer, a physicist and a mathematician find themselves in an anecdote, indeed an anecdote quite similar to many that you have no doubt already heard.

After some observations and rough calculations the engineer realizes the situation and starts laughing.

A few minutes later the physicist understands too and chuckles to herself happily as she now has enough experimental evidence to publish a paper.

This leaves the mathematician somewhat perplexed, as he had observed right away that he was the subject of an anecdote, and deduced quite rapidly the presence of humour from similar anecdotes, but considers this anecdote to be too trivial a corollary to be significant, let alone funny.

An engineer is someone who wishes he was a physicist but wasn't smart enough.

A physicist thinks if he was only a little smarter he could be God.

If God was a little smarter he could be a mathematician.

Parallel lines have so much in common… it's a shame they'll never meet.

A physicist and a mathematician were shown into a kitchen, given an empty pan, and told to boil a pint of water.

They both filled the pan with water, put it on the stove, and boiled it.

The next day they were shown into the kitchen again, given a pan full of water, and told to boil a pint of water.

The physicist took the pan, put it on the stove, and boiled it.

The mathematician took the pan and emptied it, thereby reducing it to a previously solved problem.

Why don't you do arithmetic in the jungle?

Because if you add 4+4 you get ate!

How do you solve any equation?

Multiply both sides by zero.

An opinion without 3.14159 is just an onion.

Do you know what seems odd to me?

Numbers that aren't divisible by two.

Mathematics puns are:

```
sin(madness)
```

Never discuss infinity with a mathematician, you'll never hear the end of it.

There's a fine line between numerator and denominator.

Calculus has its limits.

Why is it that the more accuracy you demand from an interpolation function, the more expensive it becomes to compute?

That's the Law of Spline Demand.

Mathematics is made of 50 percent formulas, 50 percent proofs, and 50 percent imagination.

An engineer thinks that his equations are an approximation to reality.

A physicist thinks reality is an approximation to his equations.

A mathematician doesn't care.

Mathematicians are like Frenchmen: whatever you say to them, they translate it into their own language, and forthwith it means something entirely different.

An chemist, a physicist, and a mathematician are stranded on an island when a can of food rolls ashore.

The chemist and the physicist comes up with many ingenious ways to open the can.

Then suddenly the mathematician gets a bright idea: "Assume we have a can opener..."

A mathematics professor is one who talks in someone else's sleep.

Philosophy

René Descartes walks into a bar.

The bartender says "Hey, René, gonna have your usual?"

"I don't think I am."

Descartes disappears.

There was this magnificent mathematical horse. You could teach it arithmetic which it learned with no difficulty, algebra was a breeze. It could even prove theorems in Euclidean Geometry.

When you tried to teach it Analytic Geometry however, it would rear back on its hind legs, kick ferociously neigh loudly, try to bite and generally resisted the subject.

The moral of this story is you can't put Descartes before the horse.

What do you get when you cross a joke with a rhetorical question?

Suppose there weren't any rhetorical questions?

Two philosophers are sitting by the pool.

One turns to the other and asks, "Have you read Marx?"

The other replies, "Yes, it's these damn wicker chairs."

How many existentialists does it take to change a light bulb?

Two. One to bemoan the darkness until the other redefines something else as light.

How many members of the bourgeoisie does it take to screw in a proletariat light bulb?

None. A proletariat light bulb contains the seeds of its own revolution.

Why does Pierre-Joseph Proudhon only drink herbal tea?

Because proper tea is theft.

I bought a universal remote control today.

I'm kind of afraid now...

It's hard to explain philosophy puns to kleptomaniacs, because they always take things, literally.

A linguistics professor says during a lecture that, "In English, a double negative forms a positive. But in some languages, such as Russian, a double negative is still a negative. However, in no language can a double positive form a negative."

A voice from the back of the room pipes up, "Yeah, right."

Jean-Paul Sartre is sitting at a French cafe, revising his draft of Being and Nothingness.

He says to the waitress, "I'd like a cup of coffee, please, with no cream."

The waitress replies, "I'm sorry, Monsieur, but we're out of cream. How about with no milk?"

What's the difference between an etymologist and an entomologist?

An etymologist knows the difference.

Zenophobia: the irrational fear of convergent sequences.

Who is this Rorschach guy, and why does he paint so many pictures of my parents fighting?

A fine is a tax you get when you've been doing something wrong.

A tax is a fine you get when you've been doing something right.

A Buddhist walks up to a hot dog stand and says, "Make me one with everything".

He then pays with a $20 bill and the vendor goes on to serve the next customer.

The Buddhist interrupted and said, "Hey, where's my change?"

The hot dog vendor smiled and replied, "Change must come from within!"

Why are pacifists bad at jokes?

They can't have punchlines.

Is it solipsistic in here, or is it just me?

Nihilism means nothing to me.

How did the solipsist break up with his girlfriend?

"It's not you, it's me."

Nietzsche, what's the matter?

"Nothing."

Zeno of Elea walks half way into a bar.

As you journey along the path you meet an old man.

He tells you that modern neuroscience has proved that all our actions and decisions are merely the machinations of a predetermined universe and that our concept of "free will" is naught but a comforting illusion.

If you agree with his hypothesis, **turn to page 72**

If you disagree, **turn to page 72**

The First Law of Philosophy: For every philosopher, there exists an equal and opposite philosopher.

The Second Law of Philosophy: They're both wrong.

Final Exam Question:

How do you plan on making a living with a philosophy degree?

A graduate student lends his advisor a book on tensed logic by Arthur N. Prior.

The advisor reads it, then tells his student that he dropped it off in the student's mail box.

Moments later the student returns, and breathlessly exclaims: "Professor, professor. Someone's stolen my Prior."

To which the professor sagely replies: "You're lucky around this department they haven't stolen your posterior."

Did you hear about the guy who went to the solipsist convention?

Nobody showed up.

How many philosophers does it take to change a light bulb?

It depends on how you define "change".

I'll never buy a vacuum cleaner.

It would only gather dust.

A philosophy undergraduate course is really just kidnapping done backwards.

If you don't give us a ridiculously large amount of money, we'll send you your child back.

Max Planck and Zeno of Elea get into a huge bar fight over a slight disagreement. Who won?

Planck, but not by much.

"To do is to be" - Nietzsche

"To be is to do" - Kant

"Do be do be do" - Sinatra

A philosopher is a person who knows less and less about more and more, until he knows nothing about everything.

I hate all of these philosophy puns.

I Kant stand them.

I was going to do a joke about free will.

Then I decided not to.

I love philosophy.

It really is my Nietzsche.

Existentialism?

Don't get me Sartred!

Philosophy is common sense with big words.

Immanuel Kant

But at least he tried.

Apparently Karl Marx's toilet plays music when it flushes because of the violins inherent in the cistern.

My local pub has so little class it could be a Marxist utopia.

I've finished my philosophy course.

Or have I?

I did a course on 19th century socialist thought.

I had to drop out because of poor Marx.

What do you get if you cross a philosopher with a godfather?

An offer you can't understand.

My local philosophy club has free why-fi.

Physics

A Higgs boson walks into a church.

The priest says, "We don't allow Higgs bosons in here."

The Higgs boson replies, "But how can you have mass without me?"

How many physicists does it take to change a light bulb?

Eleven. One to do it and ten to co-author the paper.

A photon is going through customs.

The customs officer asks the photon where its luggage is.

The photon answers, "I don't have any, I am traveling light."

A neutron walked into a bar and asked, "How much for a drink?"

The bartender replied, "For you, no charge."

Flying is simple. Throw yourself at the ground and miss.

Where does bad light end up?

In prism.

WANTED

Dead & Alive!

Schrödinger's cat

Schrödinger's cat walks into a bar, and doesn't.

And the bartender says, "we don't serve faster than light particles in here!"

A tachyon walks into a bar.

A seminar on time travel will be held last Tuesday.

How many theoretical physicists does it take to change a light bulb?

Two. One to hold the bulb and the other to rotate the universe.

Heisenberg and Schrödinger are out for a drive when they get stopped by the police.

The policeman asks Heisenberg, "Sir, do you know how fast you were going?"

Heisenberg replies, "No, but I know EXACTLY where I am!"

Confused, the officer says, "Sir, you were doing 80 mph," and Heisenberg throws his hands in the air and huffs, "Great, now I don't know where I am any more!"

The policeman thinks something is going on and orders the pair out of the car so that he can search it for contraband.

He looks under the seats, in the glove compartment, in the back, and then walks around the car and opens the boot.

He stares into it for a moment, turns to Schrödinger and says, "Sir, did you know there's a dead cat in here?!"

Schrödinger rolls his eyes and snorts, "Yeah, we do now!"

One physicist asks another, "What's new?"

The other replies, "C over lambda."

A hundred kilo-pascals go into a bar...

Einstein, Pascal and Newton are hanging out one afternoon.

Einstein is bored, so he suggests, "Let's play hide-and-seek. I'll be it!"

The others agree, so Einstein begins counting. "One... Two... Three..."

Pascal runs off right away to find a place to hide.

But Newton merely takes out a piece of chalk and draws a 1 metre x 1 metre square. He finishes and steps into the square just as Einstein shouts, "Ready or not – here I come!"

Einstein looks up and immediately spots Newton standing right in front of him. He says, "I found you, Newton!"

Newton replies, "No, you found Pascal."

Why does hamburger have lower energy than steak?

Because it's in the ground state.

Two cats sit on the roof of a greenhouse, which one doesn't slide off?

The one with the highest μ.

Three physicists and three chemists are on a train to a conference together.

The chemists are suprised when the physicists only buy one ticket. "How are you going to travel?" they ask.

"Wait and see," comes the reply.

On the train all three physicists pile into a bathroom.

When the conductor is checking tickets he knocks on the bathroom door and a hand shoves out the one ticket.

The chemists think this is pretty clever.

On the way home they buy one ticket for the three of them, but notice the physicists buy no ticket. "How are you going to travel?" they ask

"Wait and see," comes the reply.

On the train the three chemists pile into a bathroom.

One of the physicists walks up to the bathroom after a few minutes, knocks and says, "ticket please."

I'm not lazy, I'm overflowing with potential energy.

What do you call a one-sided go-go bar?

A Möbius strip club.

Why did the chicken cross the Möbius strip?

To get to the same side!

What's large, non-orientable and lives in the sea?

Möbius Dick.

What is the name of the first electricity detective?

Sherlock Ohms.

What did the Nuclear Physicist have for lunch?

Fission Chips.

Einstein developed a theory about space, and it was about time too!

Why are quantum physicists bad lovers?

Because when they find the position, they can't find the momentum, and when they have the momentum, they can't find the position.

I have a new theory on inertia, but it doesn't seem to be gaining momentum.

One atom says to another, "I think I've lost an electron."

The other replies, "are you sure?"

The first says, "Yes, I'm positive."

Why can't you trust atoms?

They make up everything.

What does a subatomic duck say?

Quark.

Black holes are where God divided by zero.

A physics professor has been doing an experiment, and has worked out an empirical equation that seems to explain his data. He asks the mathematics professor to look at it.

A week later, the mathematics professor says the equation is invalid. By then, the physics professor has used his equation to predict the results of further experiments, and he is getting excellent results, so he asks the mathematics professor to look again.

Another week goes by, and they meet once more. The mathematics professor tells the physics professor the equation does work, "But only in the trivial case where the numbers are real and positive."

To get to the other side.

Why did the neutrino cross the road?

What was Schrödinger's favourite movie genre?

$\psi \Phi$

The Heineken Uncertainty Principle says:

"You can never be sure how many beers you had last night."

Two theoretical physicists are lost on top of a mountain.

The first theoretical physicist pulls out a map and peruses it for a while. Then he turns to the second theoretical physicist and says: "Hey, I've figured it out. I know where we are."

"Where are we then?", says the second theoretical physicist.

"Do you see that mountain over there?", replies the first.

"Yes.", says the second.

"Well… THAT'S where we are."

A scientist was selling a microwave oven on eBay.

For sale: One ~2.45 GHz self-contained electromagnetic bombardment chamber.

Appropriate for dialectically heating polarised dihidrogen monoxide molecules by means of passing non-ionising microwave radiation through organic, non-metallic substrate within the ~122mm wavelength range.

There is a sign in Munich that reads, "Heisenberg might have slept here."

The good ship Higg was sailing through stormy seas when she foundered and was lost.

Fortunately all hands were saved except for the head of the deck crew.

The captain recorded in his log: After three days of fruitless searching we have now lost all hope of finding the Higg's bo'sun.

What's the difference between Max Factor and Quantum Theorist?

Max Factor has models that work.

Researchers in Fairbanks Alaska announced last week that they have discovered a superconductor which will operate at room temperature.

A physicist ate a meal of pasta and antipasti and exploded.

Entropy isn't what it used to be.

Air resistance is a drag.

A quantum physicist goes into a bar every night, sits down, and orders two drinks.

One he drinks himself, and the other he puts on the bar in front of the empty bar stool next to him.

After a few weeks of this, the bartender asks, "you're in here every night, and you always buy two drinks. Why do you always leave a drink in front of the empty stool?"

The physicist replies, "due to the complex laws of quantum mechanics, there's a chance that a beautiful woman will suddenly appear atop the stool. She'll see the drink and maybe we'll hit it off."

The bartender says, "But every night, the bar is full of beautiful young single women! Why not just walk up to them and ask one out? Maybe she'll say yes."

To which the physicist responds, "yeah, but what's the chance of **that** ?"

Theoretical Physics is a science locally isomorphic to Mathematics.

Wave if you've met Schrödinger!

A wife walks in on her husband, a string theorist, in bed with another woman.

"Wait!", he exclaims, "I can explain everything!"

Curiosity may or may not have killed the cat.

I have a really good quantum physics joke, but you can only know either what the joke is **or** how funny it is.

If you aren't confused by quantum physics, then you haven't really understood it.

What happens when electrons lose their energy?

They get Bohr'ed.

If you tied buttered toast to the back of a cat and dropped it from a height in a closed box, what would happen?

Pseudoscience

A homeopath forgot to take his medicine.

He died of an overdose.

Homeopathy is safe to practise at home.

There's nothing to it.

How many homeopaths does it take to change a light bulb?

0.000000000000000000000000000001

I used to take this great homeopathic remedy for my stomach problems.

But then I heard it passed a double-blind placebo controlled study, so I stopped taking it.

One of the great things about homeopathy is that because the remedies don't actually do anything there's no need to worry about nasty side effects.

A politician is waiting anxiously for election results. He finally hears he's lost and collapses.

His acolytes rush to summon his homeopath, who enters and starts questioning them about the modalities of the illness.

"He lost the election," they say, "and just collapsed."

"Lost by what margin", asks the homeopath.

"Oh, some 4000-5000 votes", they reply.

"FOUR thousand or FIVE thousand? How can I prescribe unless you tell me THAT?"

Homeopathy is actually an effective cure for dehydration.

"No officer, this heroin is just a preservative for my homeopathic remedy."

"There's nothing but heroin in here, son."

"You don't understand how homeopathy works!"

The lack of evidence homeopathically PROVES that homeopathy works.

What's the difference between a sociopath and a homeopath.

Homeopaths have killed more people.

Did you hear about the suicidal homeopath?

He took 1/50th of the recommended dose.

Did you hear about the homeopathic terrorist?

He had an evil plan to poison the world by dropping a molecule of glucose into the ocean.

I'm into crystal healing.

It's a pyrite's life for me.

May the quartz be with you.

One woman to another in a crystal shop:

"I just bought some really cool eye shadow for my Third Eye!"

Well, you passed the polygraph test.

Welcome to sales.

Anyone who believes in phrenology should have their head examined.

I believe in phrenology.

A phrenologist once checked the bumps on my head and successfully concluded that I was accident prone.

He says he doesn't believe in astrology?

But he would say that because his Mercury is in Capricorn.

Horoscopes are a bunch of nonsense.

Horoscope: You're lonely and tired.

Astrology is 100% real!

Unless I don't agree with it.

So what do you do?

I'm currently trying to eliminate all Cancers.

Wow, impressive.

Then I'll move on to Virgos.

I don't believe in astrology.

I'm a Sagittarian, and we're sceptical.

I'm a typical Capricorn;

I'm hard working, loyal, sometimes stubborn and I don't believe in astrology.

U.N. experts are saying that climate change could start threatening the world's supply of fruits and vegetables.

Then Americans said, "OK, let us know when it starts affecting Twinkies and Hot Pockets."

Why did the climate change denier cross the road?

It was just a natural cycle.

How many climate sceptics does it take to change a light bulb?

None. It's too early to say if the light bulb needs changing.

Why are surfers our best chance for solving climate change?

Buildings sticking out of the surf get in the way of a good wave.

How many politicians does it take to solve climate change?

The theory that politicians solve anything at all is yet to be proven.

I never thought I'd buy into Feng Shui

But oh how the tables have turned.

Feng Shui is Mandarin Chinese for

Put your husband's stuff in the garage.

Studying Feng Shui has really opened doors for me.

I moved my computer off my desk.

You wouldn't understand. It's a Feng Shui thing and it has successfully reduced my work related stress.

My ex wife is a Feng Shui consultant.

She must be good because she cleared out all of my possessions and I don't have to worry about money any more.

What did the farmer use to make crop circles?

A protractor.

Scientists have just deciphered the alien message in a crop circle.

It said take me to your weeder.

What do you call a yeti with a six-pack?

An abdominal snowman.

Sci-Fi and Fantasy

How many ears does Spock have?

Three: the left ear, the right ear - and the final front ear.

What do you call a smuggler who has been frozen in carbonite?

A hardened criminal.

Kirk, Spock, McCoy and Ensign Ricky are beaming down to a strange new planet.

Guess who's not coming back.

How can Daleks tell each other apart?

Thay. Jast. Caan.

How many Borg does it take to change a light bulb?

All of them.

An Ewok strolls into a bar and says to the bartender, "I'll have a whisky and ...... soda."

The bartender says, "Sure thing, but why the little pause?"

"Dunno," says the Ewok. "I've had them all my life."

Two Jawas walk under a bar.

Two weeping angels go into a bar.

The first one turns to the other and asks, "How are you doing?"

The other looks round and they both say, nothing...

A Silence walks into...

A clone trooper walks into a pub and asks the barman, "Hey, have you seen my brother?"

I dunno," says the barman, "What does he look like?"

Why did the Borg cross the road?

Because it assimilated the chicken!

Very funny, Scotty. Now beam down my clothes.

We have engaged the Borg.

The wedding will be Friday.

Why did episodes 4, 5, and 6 come before 1, 2, and 3?

Because in charge of directing, Yoda was.

What do you call a Jedi who knows how to Photoshop?

Adobe Wan Kenobi.

Why is The Force like duct tape?

It has a light side, a dark side, and it binds the galaxy together.

What happens when The Doctor goes back in time and sees himself?

You get a pair-a-docs!

Why did the Dalek cross the road?

To exterminate humanity.

And the barman says "Sorry, we don't serve time travellers."

The Doctor walks into a pub.

Luke, you've switched off your targeting computer. Is something wrong?

Yeah, it uses Apple Maps.

Son: "What are you having for dinner Dad?"

Dad: "Wookie steak."

Son: "Is it any good?"

Dad: "It's a little Chewy..."

Why do Imperial Stormtroopers use iPhones?

Because they couldn't find the Droid they were looking for.

Which bounty hunter has money problems?

Bobba Debt.

Why did Darth Vader hate father's day?

Because everyone bought him a TIE.

The real Star Wars back story:

A guy can only be called "Little Orphan Annie" so many times before he snaps!

What do you call Stormtroopers playing Monopoly?

Game of Clones.

Lukewarm:

A Jedi who couldn't find the thermostat.

Why can't you enter Sauron's lair?

Because no matter how many you open, there is always Mordor!

My Professor was called Gandalf.

He didn't let me pass.

I would make another Lord Of the Rings joke,

but all the good ones Aragorn.

What do you call the wraith king?

A ring leader!

What to the Orcs around Lorien fear the most?

Elf-inflicted wounds.

Tolkien is Hobbit forming.

A Nazgûl walks into a bar.

The barman says, "I'm sorry, we don't serve your kind in here."

The Nazgûl replies, "That's Wraithist."

Two Nazgûl walk into a bar.

One says, "Screeeeeechooooooowwwwwwoooooo'

The other says,"I heard that one already."

Two elves walk into a bar

The hobbit laughs and walks under it

Those jokes have a familiar ring to them.

Last night I dreamed I was the author of Lord of the Rings.

I was Tolkien in my sleep.

Statistics

There are two types of people in this world:

Those who can extrapolate from incomplete data.

A statistician is someone who is good with numbers but lacks the personality to be an accountant.

A statistician is someone who tells you, when you've got your head in the fridge and your feet in the oven, that you are, on average, very comfortable.

Three statisticians are out hunting.

Suddenly, a deer appears 50 yards away.

The first statistician shoots and hits the tree 5 feet to the left.

The second statistician shoots and hits the tree 5 feet to the right.

The third statistician starts jumping up and down, yelling "We got him! We got him!"

Why did the statistician drown while crossing a river?

It was 3 feet deep… on average

Why did the student get upset when his teacher called him average?

It was a mean thing to say!

Latest survey shows that 3 out of 4 people make up 75% of the world's population.

Have you heard the latest statistics joke?

Probably.

If you live to be one hundred, you've got it made. Very few people die past that age.

Statistics play an important role in genetics. For instance, statistics prove that numbers of offspring is an inherited trait. If your parent didn't have any kids, odds are you won't either.

A statistician friend of mine travels a lot for his job. I often run into him in airports or on planes.

One day I run into him on a train. "Sam," I say, "why aren't you on a plane?"

"Joe," he says, "I figured out the odds of there being a bomb on a plane. While the risk is quite low (1 in 1.5 million), that is still higher than I am willing to accept. Now I travel by train."

Two weeks go by and when I take a plane to the coast, there sits Sam on the plane. "Sam," I say, "I thought you had said that 1 in 1.5 million was too great a risk for you."

"Joe," Sam says, "you are right: 1 in 1.5 million IS too risky for me."

"But Sam," I say, "why are you on the plane?"

"Well, Joe, I went home and calculated the odds of there being TWO bombs on the same plane. Those odds are much slimmer. Now I just bring my own bomb!"

A statistician is a person who draws a mathematically precise line from an unwarranted assumption to a foregone conclusion.

Eighty percent of all people consider themselves to be above average.

A physicist, a chemist, and a statistician are called in to see their dean.

Just as they arrive the dean is called out of his office, leaving the three professors there.

The professors see with alarm that there is a fire in the waste basket.

The physicist says, "We must cool down the materials until their temperature is lower than the ignition temperature and then the fire will go out."

The chemist says, "No! No! We must cut off the supply of oxygen so that the fire will go out due to lack of one of the reactants."

While the physicist and chemist are debating, they observe with alarm that the statistician is running around the room starting other fires.

They both scream, "What are you doing?" To which the statistician replies, "Trying to get an adequate sample size."

If there is a 50-50 chance that something can go wrong, then 9 times out of ten it will.

40% of sick days are used on Monday and Friday.

Two statisticians were travelling in an aircraft from LA to New York. About an hour into the flight, the pilot announced that they had lost an engine, but don't worry, there are three left. However, instead of 5 hours it would take 7 hours to get to New York.

A little later, he announced that a second engine failed, and they still had two left, but it would take 10 hours to get to New York.

Somewhat later, the pilot again came on the intercom and announced that a third engine had died. Never fear, he announced, because the plane could fly on a single engine. However, it would now take 18 hours to get to New York.

At this point, one statistician turned to the other and said, "Gee, I hope we don't lose that last engine, or we'll be up here forever!"

Patient: "Will I survive this risky operation?"

Surgeon: "Yes, I'm absolutely sure that you will survive the operation."

Patient: "How can you be so sure?"

Surgeon: "Well 9 out of 10 patients die in this operation, and yesterday my ninth patient died."

"Why are you leaving? You only moved to this lovely neighbourhood a few weeks ago."

"Yes, but I read in the local paper a bit of statistics that said, 'most vehicle accidents happen within eight miles of your home'."

Did you know that 87.166253% of all statistics claim a precision of results that is not justified by the method employed?

Here are the results of our drug testing study on rabbits: 1/3 of the sample died; 1/3 of the sample survived; the other one ran away.

It is proven that the celebration of birthdays is healthy.

Statistics show that those people who celebrate the most birthdays become the oldest.

A statistician was asked how her husband was.

She replied "Compared with whom?"

You Might Be a Statistician if:

- no one wants your job.
- you are right 95% of the time.
- you feel complete and sufficient.
- you found accountancy too exciting.
- you never have to say you are certain.
- you may not be normal but you are transformable.

Did you hear about the statistician who drank too much?

He got kurtosis of the liver.

Bad statistics jokes aren't normally distributed.

Teenage pregnancy rates reduce dramatically after the age of nineteen.

How many statisticians does it take to change a light bulb?

One (plus or minus three).

85.7142857% of dwarves aren't Happy.

Regression is a powerful tool for forecasting.

Economists using it successfully predicted ten out of the last two recessions.

Don't become a novelist; be a statistician, as there's much more scope for the imagination.

Statisticians often find it difficult to live within their means.

Statisticians:

Weapons of maths deduction.

Actuary:

Someone who didn't think statistics was already boring enough and decided to combine it with insurance.

Variance:

What any two statisticians are at.

More than 95% of all violent crimes are committed within 24 hours of drinking water.

We must bring an end to the water menace!

The Vatican City has 5.9 Popes per square mile.

Mandelbrot once said he was born in Poland and educated in France, making him German, on average.

Did you hear about the politician who promised that, if he was elected, he'd make certain that everybody would get an above average income?

Are statisticians normal?

Look on the bright side – you're in the top 90% of the class!

I'm right 97% of the time, so who cares about the other 4%?

Printed in Great Britain
by Amazon